Salt or Sugar

ISBN 10: 0692967451

ISBN 13: 978-0692967454

these words are for
the eyes that see them
and the hearts that feel them

in loving memory
of my love

i always wanted you
with no strings attached
because i knew
those same strings
would ruin you one day

i feel like the saddest
and loneliest person on the planet
i wish you were keeping me company
instead of my memories of you

i used to think
that being selfless
was a noble
and honorable
characteristic
but fuck that
Ms. Lorde was right

   — a nod to Audre Lorde on self care / my much
      wiser self

' i'm okay'

— a lie i compulsively tell everyone

i was convinced
that depression
would eat me alive
like acid burning
through flesh
but i'm still here
alive

i still compulsively check my phone
waiting to see your name
across my screen
then i realize
that i'll never
receive another message
from you

with me
you never knew
if you'd get salt
or sugar for the day
but you'd take a taste anyway
and either way you stayed
you saw the best
in everything
you always knew
how to make salt
taste like sugar

out of all the eyes
i've met
yours always
made me feel
the prettiest

i know you can't
make homes
out of people
but where else
is love
supposed to live?

— homeless

you've always been the sun
and i am a moon
our love will forever
be my favorite
eclipse

it's truly okay
not to be okay
and not knowing
when you will be
is okay too

i hope your back
no longer aches
i felt the weight
of the stories
you carried

you saw me better
than any mirror
could show me
myself

speak your truth
until your voice cracks
and if you have to whisper
that's impactful too

i didn't recognize strength
until i realized how easily
i could piece myself together
after falling apart

i mourn
the lives
that were lost
but
i mourn
the hearts
that loved them
even more

don't let anyone
convince you
that your
power
solely lies
between
your legs
it's between
your ears
and between
your teeth

— free game

it's amazing
how the tongue
can touch the roof
of your mouth
and spew words
sharp enough
to penetrate bones
but also can
spill words that can
heal and ease
every scar and wound
like they never existed

— single edged sword

i started living
when you died
to distract myself
from the fact that
this pair is now
just one

i refuse to talk about you in past tense

i'll go
wherever you are
it'll just take me a while
to get to you now

each day
it feels like it's only
been one day
since i haven't spoken to you
but it's been 107 days
and counting

after 305 days
i thought my body
would stop
producing tears
it hasn't

you know
it's love
when it feels like
the world
doesn't exist
outside
of the arms
that hold you

am i alive
if you aren't?

i attended your funeral
but really it felt like
mine too

how many times will i drown
to save you?
each time i lie lifeless
in a pool of tears
then revived
with a whispered 'thank you'
only to do it all over again
i have no more lifelines
i'm all out of tries
if i keep saving you
who will save me?

why must you show up uninvited?

— depression and her sister, grief

only the night
can get my heart
and my mind
in the same place
at the same time

i know that if there's no rain
there will be no flowers
but i have enough bouquets

— a series of unfortunate events

if i ever told you
how i truly felt
about those strings
i knew you'd never
forgive me
so i never did

the nighttime reminds me of you
because it's when we were
our true selves
unveiled

he admired how beautiful
she was when she was naked
not the times when
he saw her bare skin
or the times when
he'd undress her
with his eyes
but the moments when
she'd unfasten her thoughts
and spill whatever
was in her heart
into his hands

maybe our plans were built on sand

SOS

love yourself
so deeply
that it
offends
those who don't
deserve you

— true first love

you're never lonely
when you drink alone
you're accompanied
by the thoughts
you always ignore

if the world goes up in flames
i want to sit on the moon
and watch it set ablaze
with you

of course
my skin is thick
it's been through
many storms
and survived
the end of the world
multiple times

— resilience

all of our broken pieces make a complete picture

i tend to ruin things
because i am a phoenix
that rises from destruction
that's all i know

i can't keep track
of my mind these days
it's been gone for 73 days
maybe i'll find it
wherever i'll find you
all my thoughts are about you

my thoughts are as heavy
as the bags under my eyes
from the nights i've cried
my heart is heavy
from taking on others' pain
and struggles
and making them my own
i'll be my own redemption
i just have to remind myself:
pack lighter
run faster

SOS

can you take a day off, please?

— grief

the moon
has always
kept my secrets
my heart sheds itself
whenever she's present

— nocturnal

it's okay
let it out
let it all out
you'll need
that water
for growth

— tears / blooming gardens

i'll never be a damsel in distress
i'll always save myself

the bayou floods through my veins
washed over by the Pacific coast
despite being kissed by the California sun
you loved me and treated me
as if my skin was baked
by the southern humidity
what a love it was to know you
it could take an hour to walk you down the steps
as it would to give a way a bride
but really it was the honor of being trusted
the honor and trust of letting
those you've birthed
guide you
just as you've always done
and continue to do

— momo (grandma)

if i die
we can get married
at the gates of heaven
like lovers do
like angels do

i got a thing for J's
Justin, Jameson
and Jack are my faves
i know it's a good time
when i hear those names

because of you
i know
what love
looks
feels
tastes
and sounds like

my mother always say
nobody's perfect
and that those who are perfect
are angels in heaven
maybe that's why
you aren't here

tears are just wet secrets

you don't have to be
who you say you are
as long as
i can know you
the real you
that isn't shown
to everyone else

— we all pretend sometimes

my crown is heavier
than the problems i bear
but i keep it lifted

i've been told
that i now have to reserve
a space in my heart
for you
but i don't have it
i gave it to you a decade ago
and it was buried with you

only you
could ignite fires
within me
put them out
and not get burned

oblivion gets me through the days

dealing with a sudden loss
is like reaching the peak
of a rollercoaster
and staying there
without reaching the bottom
like waiting for the best part
of your favorite song to come on
but it never plays

i am dealing with it
by not dealing with it

i immortalize you
with words
so you
can live
outside my heart

our love will outlive us

our strength
is embedded
in our melanin
and coils in our hair
how can we not be strong?
how can we not be resilient?
we are seeds
watered by generations
of mothers' sweat
tears and perseverance

— women of color

we fall in love
although we know
we're just visiting
but it'll always
make the stay
worthwhile

— lifetime

how do you harm someone
like they belong to no one?

nothing feels
the same
since you're
no longer
on my skin

i was told that loved ones
come to visit in dreams
have you not shown up
because you know
this is a nightmare?

blue is my favorite color
and it's yours too
when you left
i became obsessed with it
maybe because
it's also
a reflection of how
i feel

just as you left
i hope you return

sometimes
i dislike silence
it gives my thoughts
an opportunity to be louder
than they already are

pain:
a catalyst
for the constructive
or the destructive

i spell love with all of the letters in your name

i've ran myself dry
from pouring
and pouring
love
with hopes
that you'd be satisfied
and your heart
would be overfilled
but i learned
that i was pouring
and pouring
into a bottomless pit

— when it's never enough

i'm sorry
that i can't give you
the love
that you sought
from everyone else
i'm sorry
that i can't teach you
how to give the love
you never found
but i can tell you
that this love
all of this love you wanted
wasn't in the places
you've looked
you've been harvesting it
and it should have been
invested in yourself
all along

i find comfort
in a room full of strangers
it saves me the time
of answering
insincere questions
with honest answers

existing
is not
the same
as living

i never wanted
to see you
in a box
but i visit you
every Saturday
anyway

don't believe anyone
who says you are
too tough
too difficult
or too anything
to be loved
because
roses
have thorns
too

— you can be strong and delicate / you are
always worthy of being loved

i looked forward
to the day we got married
i already knew
what my vows would say
but little did i know
that i would use those words
for your obituary

i used to eat my words
until my stomach churned
for others' comfort
only to vomit them all
out when i was fed
up with being unwell
i don't swallow words
anymore
my words
whatever they may be
are for whomever needs them
whenever they need them
if my words make them unwell
that is their discomfort to deal with
not mine

— honesty

no one likes lonely
but she is wise
she'll always teach you
things about yourself
that you wouldn't learn
with someone else

i've been bending
and not breaking
but internally
parts of me
are splintering
but i keep bending

— vulnerability

women often become mothers
without having children
though we can birth a nation
this divine ability
comes with unfair expectations
we are taught to be selfless
and take care of others
all while disregarding ourselves
we are expected to dim our lights
so others can shine
we piece things together
when others fall short
we are women
we are human
we have the right
to just be ourselves
and nothing or
no one else
we have the right
to not render our time
effort or energy
to anyone

my love has started to feel like a museum
i stare at you through a glass
i search through your things
each time it feels like a new experience
i feel and relive stories
by touching the things you left behind
just like we do when we go to a museum
we glare at things
that once belonged to someone
we glare at things
that was once loved by someone

SOS

i looked for a truth
or a cure
in the bottles
i've emptied
but
the only truth
i found
was that
it wasn't
just the bottles
that were empty

— sober

88

when i need a place to hide
i get lost in our secrets

when my eyes
greet the moon
my heart howls
for you

you don't touch things that don't belong to you
didn't your mother tell you?
how dare you touch parts of my heart
if you don't want it?
how dare you hold my body
like you own it?
then when i seek this comfort consistently
you abandon it all
like you don't want it
there's a name for people like you:
thief
there's a place for people like you:
hell

there could be freedom in destruction

best friends are sturdy
reliable walls
that build you up
after every break down

— thankful

behind the biggest hearts
are patches and stitches
from previous damages

don't let
silence
start riots
inside you

— the unsaid

i know something in your body
is trying to destroy you
but it cannot not destroy your spirit
it cannot touch your impenetrable soul
give it hell as it has given you and your body
strength will always outlast struggle

i wish it didn't take me
so long to realize
that i cannot fix things
that i did not break
and that fixing things
is not my responsibility

ever think about
how far a tear
has traveled?
from the mind
sparked by an emotion
orchestrated from the heart
through the tear glands
to spill from the eye
and land on your cheek
hand, tissue or whatever else
you use to wipe it away
that is quite a journey
to not acknowledge it
or try to conceal it
it will always be okay
to cry

i'll probably cry for you eternally, internally

heartstrings
aren't made
for symphonies
don't play
with emotions
always leave
when things
aren't in tune

strangers
can have
the same
blood

— relatives who are distant

you are special
if i let you disrupt
my solitude
so use your manners
this space
isn't for everyone

i'm learning
to let go of things
that drown me
i'll never
stay afloat
if i'm always
willing to be
an anchor

appreciate the dreamer
who doesn't sleep

— the hustle

the world keeps moving
even when yours
has been snatched
from beneath your feet
but as the world moves
you will too
when you're ready

— morning / mourning

who you are
and who
you will become
will meet
and when they do
you will appreciate
the journey

— reminders

you brought me flowers
without acknowledging
that you were one
too

and if i ever
love(d) you
i mean it

— one does not unlove

i've taken so many vacations
in effort to escape
my feelings
each time
i packed everything
but emotional baggage
to bring with me
but there are only
so many flights
i can catch

i'm holding on to you with every part of me

the heart remembers
what the mind
wants to forget

i've grown weary
from being cloaked
with sadness
dolled up with
a painted on face
stamped with a
socially acceptable smile
i need new attire

we have been
magicians
since birth

— black women

i have my father's temper
and my mother's heart
i am the calm
and i am the storm

i hope you get nine lives
and spend them all
with me

who
spilled
salt
on the year?

— superstitions

don't pick yourself apart
to appease anyone else
see yourself through
your own mirror
and no one else's

there's a difference
between using
love
as a reason
and using
love
as an excuse

i bloom in darkness
i am not difficult
i have a beauty
that isn't seen
by everyone

— moon flower

take breaks
to break
shattered pieces
are strong
too

cry it out
scream it out
sweat it out
write it out
just get it
out

— breaking bottled emotions

don't be afraid
of storms
become one

give your thoughts
another home
they don't
have to stay
in your head

— therapy / creativity / the release

sweet nothings
feel good
and taste good
but
they'll never be filling
without actions
behind them

— don't starve yourself

drive
will get you
anywhere
on empty

dress yourself in love
it'll always look
good on you

i'd carry you
until my knees bled
from dragging
them against the ground
but then i realized
that i had to stop
walking miles
for someone
who was never
willing
to clean my
wounds

maybe heaven
is closer
than we think
and the stars
are just the
glistening souls
of our loved ones
left to guide us

do not ask me
'what's wrong?'
as you watch me
clean debris
from under my fingernails
after dusting off
your heart
for the umpteenth time
while mine dangles
from my chest

SOS

try to snip us
we will
continue to grow
wildly

— roots / resistance

your tongue is burnt
from kissing lovers
who've lied to you
and didn't mean
you any good
sprinkle sugar on it
douse yourself
with sugar
sugar heals
wounds

SOS

i don't cry over spilled milk
it's just upsetting to know
that you're not willing
to help clean up
a mess
that we made together

we took all of the chips
that we carried on our shoulders
and built a fortress
where nothing or
no one else mattered
we thought this place was secure
because we used our hearts
as keys
but little did i know
the walls we built
were penetrable

— i wish i could've saved you

sometimes i regret
that i'll only
be able to
give birth
to these words
for you

my mother says i should pray
to get this monkey off my back
but she doesn't understand
that it has become my pet
and only companion

— anger mixed with grief

you can find peace
while in pieces
sometimes
we need to break
to find
what we've
buried
inside us
to relieve us

in solitude
i still feel your breath
grazing my skin
and i still hear
the sounds of secrets
whistling past your lips

you are my piece of peace

i looked in the mirror once and saw your face
i saw the pain
and the scars you wear
i picked up my foundation brush
and as i put on my makeup
i painted on the smile you always gave
when you were broken
and felt belittled and ashamed
but you were always brave
you were always beautiful
you were always loving
you were always strong
the pain you harvested was fueled
by your fear of being weak and helpless
but you always had courage
when i look in the mirror
i see you
i am brave
i am beautiful
i am loving
i am strong
because of you

— splitting image

be proud of your scars
you've survived something

scars tell the stories
that our hearts carry

broken
doesn't
mean
irreparable

— heal

you'll always know
who truly loves you
especially
during the times
when it feels like
even love
doesn't love you

something good
can come
from darkness
even vanilla is black
in its natural state

if you can find your way
through darkness
you can make it
anywhere
you're all the light
you need
when you can't find it

salt will get in your wounds
only if you let it
replace it with sugar
and see how much
you'll heal

With lots of encouragement, I became fearless and decided to let my heart bleed through ink that was then turned into words pressed on paper.

You've reached the end.

Thank you for feeling with me.

Special acknowledgements:

I firmly believe that we stand on the shoulders of those who've come before us. So, I'd like to thank Nayyirah Waheed, Warsan Shire, Rupi Kaur, Amanda Lovelace and many other poets who brilliantly and passionately write poems that are touching and inspiring. I am moved by your work and inspired by you all.

I thank my best friends who took time to read these poems and handle them with care. I thank you all infinitely for giving me the courage to actually share my intimate thoughts and feelings with others.

Many, many thanks to Morris. Thank you for being family and thank you for designing this amazing cover for the book.

Lastly, I thank my beloved Justin for always believing in me and being my muse.

About the writer:

Ida is a proud introvert, feminist and aunt from Oakland, CA. She enjoys DIY projects, traveling and live music shows. She has an affinity for art (music and literature in particular), tacos, and baked goods. Ida discovered her love and appreciation for poetry at a young age. She then began to intimately write poems as a means to document her emotions. She's also not the best at talking about herself. Ida has a M.A. in Applied Anthropology from San José State University and a B.S. in Anthropology from UC Riverside. *Salt or Sugar* is her first published collection of poetry.

About the book:

Salt or Sugar is a collection of poetry about pain, grief, love and strength. The poems highlight bitter and sad experiences in life, happier and sweeter experiences and bittersweet moments. Each poem is left to the interpretation of the reader to decide if it is about salt (bitter and sad experiences), sugar (happier and sweeter experiences) or the mixture of the two.

www.ingramcontent.com/pod-product-compliance
Lightning Source LLC
Chambersburg PA
CBHW060323050426
42449CB00011B/2623